FIRST CODING

ONLINE SAFETY

By Sam Thompson

BookLife PUBLISHING

©2020
BookLife Publishing Ltd.
King's Lynn
Norfolk PE30 4LS

A catalogue record for this book is available from the British Library.

ISBN: 978-1-83927-235-6

All facts, statistics, web addresses and URLs in this book were verified as valid and accurate at time of writing. No responsibility for any changes to external websites or references can be accepted by either the author or publisher.

Written by:
Sam Thompson

Edited by:
Madeline Tyler

Designed by:
Dan Scase

ONLINE SAFETY

Photo credits

All images are courtesy of Shutterstock.com. With thanks to Getty Images, Thinkstock Photo and iStockphoto. Front cover – magic pictures, DG-Studio, Samuel Borges Photography, RoryDesign, the_same_space, Lineicons freebird, Happy Art, RaulAlmu. 4&5 – Phil's Mommy, Photographee.eu. 6&7 – Kylie Walls, Jevanto Productions. 8&9 – Rawpixel.com, Tero Vesalainen. 10&11 – mangpor2004, Nicescene. 12&13 – Rawpixel.com, AngieYeoh. 14&15 – fizkes, Rawpixel.com, snowsplendid. 16&17 – Rawpixel.com, Rido. 18&19 – LightField Studios, Sue Tansirimas, Lyudmyla Kharlamova. 20&21 – metamorworks, jamesteohart. 22&23 – Victuallers, Paul Clarke. Background on all pages – magic pictures. Tablet – Olga Lebedeva. Icons – RoryDesign, the_same_space, Lineicons freebird, Happy Art, RaulAlmu.

CONTENTS

Words that look like this can be found in the glossary on page 24.

WHAT IS CODING?

Coding means telling a computer what to do by writing a set of <u>instructions</u>. The set of instructions is called a code. We use coding to do all sorts of amazing things on a computer.

Another name for coding is programming.

A computer is a machine that can follow instructions and <u>store</u> information.

Information is the numbers and facts that tell you about something.

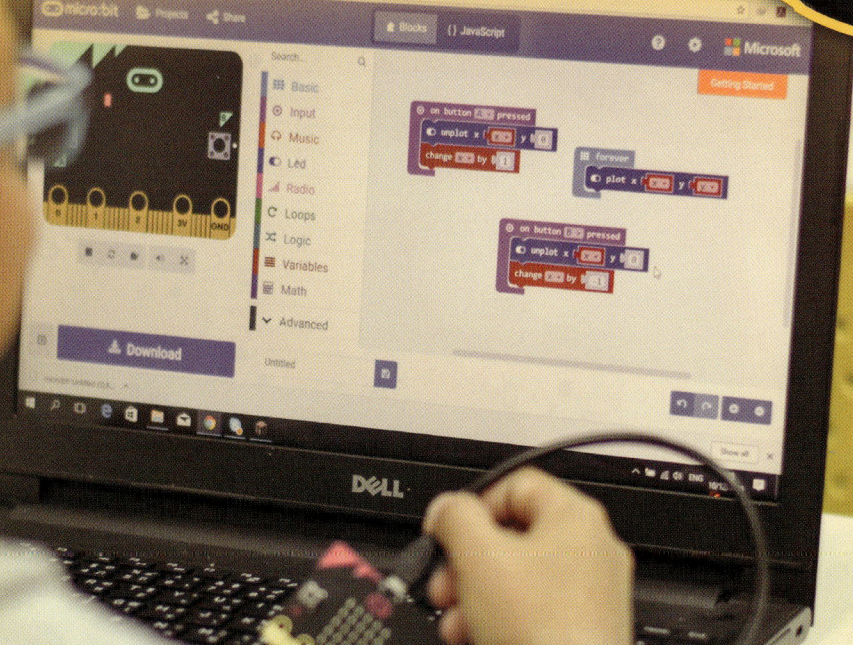

Someone who writes code is called a programmer.

Bits of information are put together to make a program. The program is then <u>run</u> on a computer.

WHAT IS PRIVACY?

In the world of computers, privacy is about making sure that not everyone can see all your information. When it comes to the internet, privacy is very important.

Keeping some things private is not the same as having a secret. Privacy means that only people you trust know this information, and nobody else can see it.

READ THE PRIVACY POLICY

The security of your data is extremely important to us. Thank you for trusting your trust in Panasonic.

Kind Regards

... information correcte
...of your data, revoke
...rights or ask for data portability

Privacy is meant to keep you safe.

PERSONAL INFORMATION

Personal information is the information that not everyone should see. The only people who should see personal information are people you trust, such as your family, carer, teacher or very close friends.

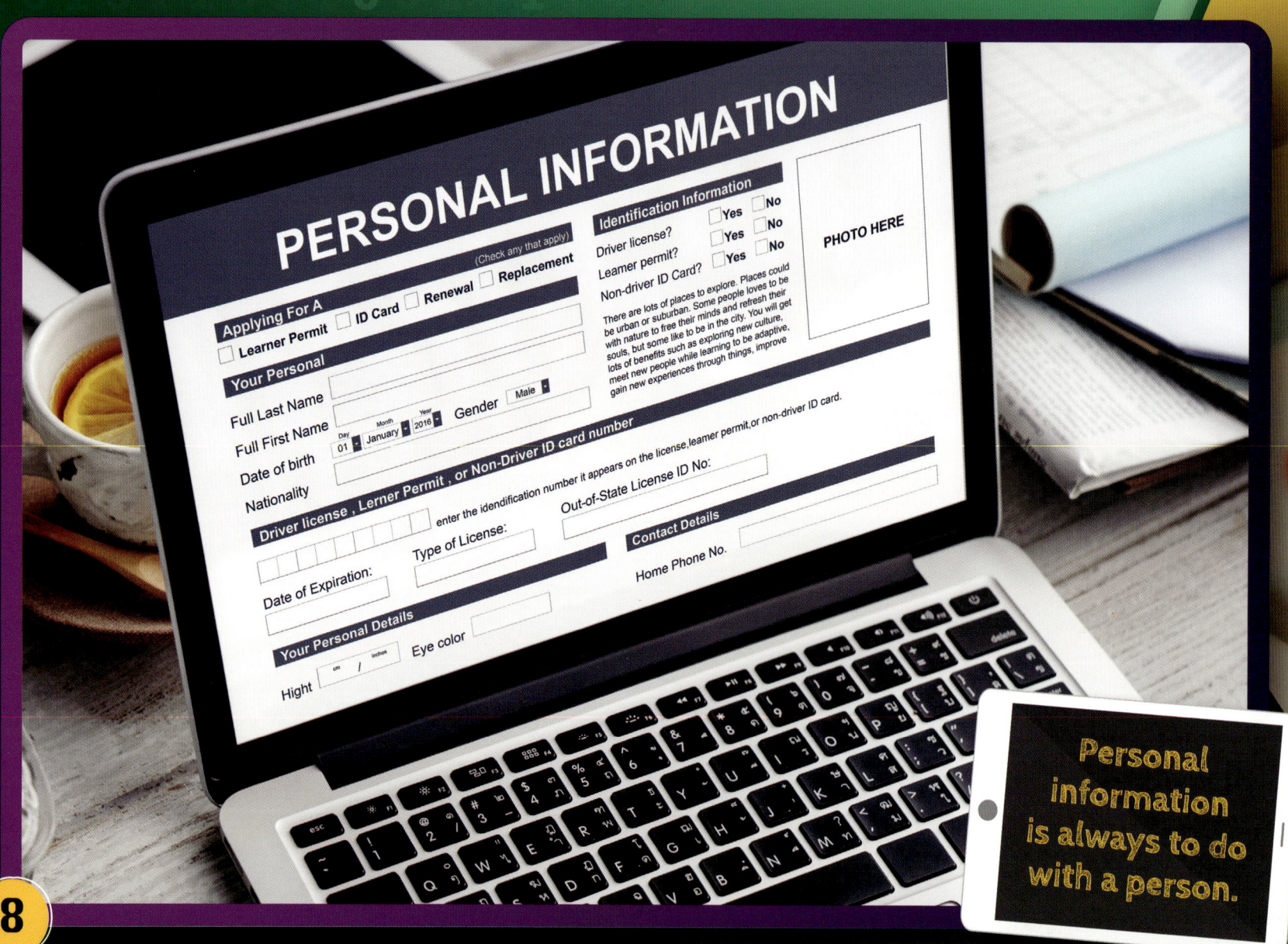

Personal information is always to do with a person.

Here are some examples
of personal information:

- Name
- Home address
- Email address
- Phone number
- Birthday
- Password
- Your photograph
- Medical information

9

PASSWORDS

A password is used to keep your information and <u>accounts</u> safe. A password is like a key. People cannot use your information or accounts without your password.

Here are some tips for making a safe password:

- Use a mixture of letters, numbers and <u>symbols</u>
- Don't use the same password for everything
- Try not to write down your passwords

PASSWORD GENERATOR

Letters	Numbers	Symbols
Baboolean	45	@
Code	000	?
FirstCoding	**123**	**!**
BeingSafe	101	>>
TheFixer	99	()

This is just one way to make a password. You can use any words, numbers and symbols in any order you want.

11

YOUR DATA

Data is another word for information. Sometimes you might have to put your data online. For example, you usually need to give an email address when signing up to a website.

Login

ENTER
click here for more information

Some websites might ask for your birthday and name too.

You shouldn't give your data to websites you don't trust. You should also be careful about putting your data online in places that everyone can see, such as on <u>social media</u>.

If you do put data on social media or on a website, make sure it is private. Setting something to private means you can control who sees it.

SAFE WEBSITES

You should try to stay on websites you trust. If you aren't sure which websites are safe, ask an adult for help.

Here are some well-known, trusted websites:

- www.natgeokids.com/uk/
- www.sesamestreet.org/
- www.bbc.co.uk/history/forkids/
- nhm.ac.uk (Natural History Museum - full of dinosaurs!)

It can be dangerous to go on websites you haven't heard of before. You might see something that upsets you. You should only visit websites that you know are safe.

You might have a <u>filter</u> on your internet at school and at home. This can help you stay safe.

SAFETY ON THE INTERNET

The internet is a great way to talk to people from all over the world. However, remember that not everyone is who they say they are.

Sometimes people lie on the internet.

Always tell your parents or carers about the people you talk to online. You should never go alone to meet up with someone you met online. Take an adult that you trust with you.

CYBERBULLYING

When someone is bullied online, it is called cyberbullying. It can be very upsetting to be cyberbullied, or to see it happen to other people.

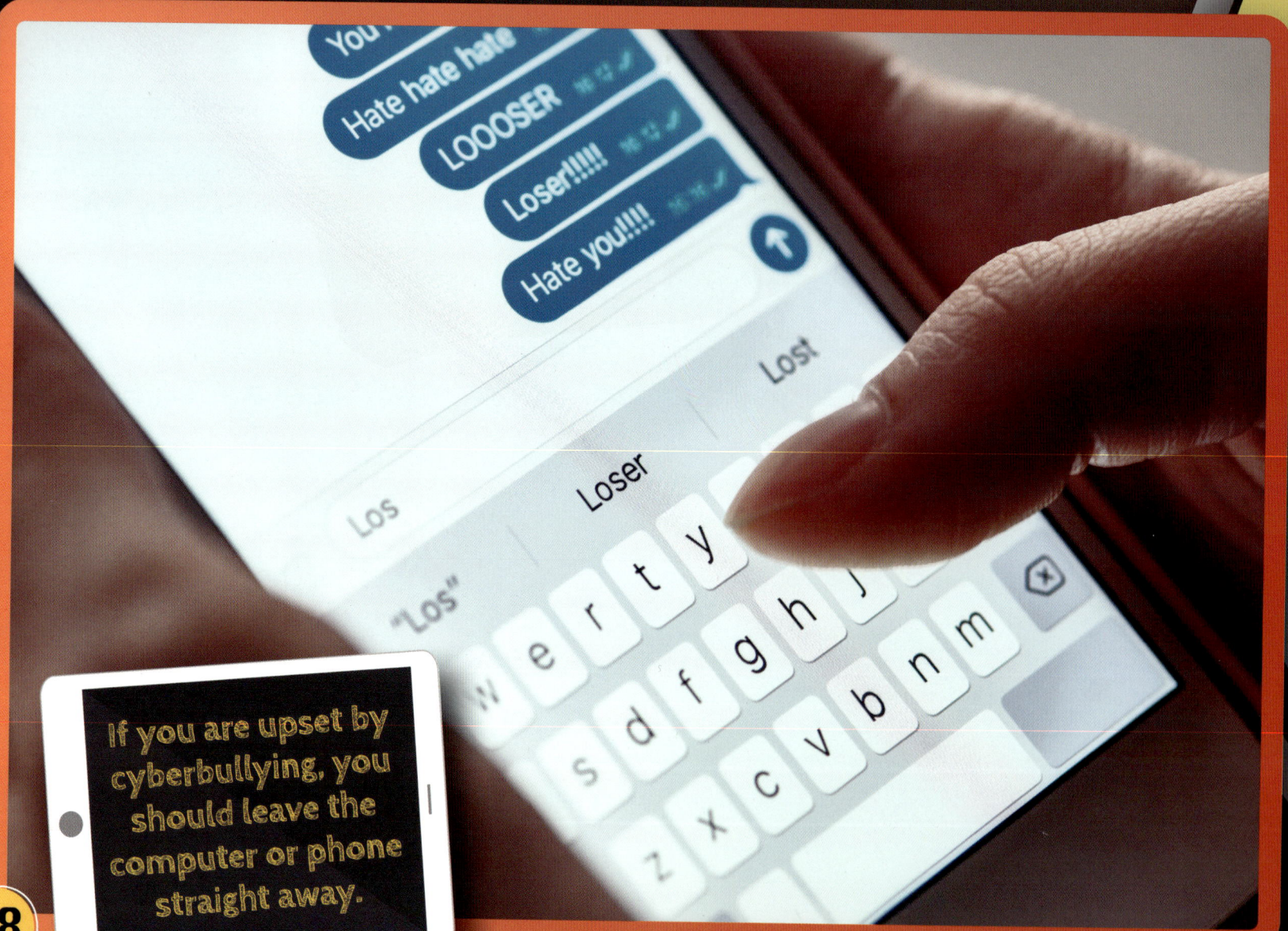

If you are upset by cyberbullying, you should leave the computer or phone straight away.

If you are upset by cyberbullying, it is important that you tell an adult about it. Never join in with cyberbullying, even if people online want you to.

Cyberbullying can come from strangers or even friends on the internet.

WHAT CAN CODING DO?

Coding can do amazing things in the real world. Many countries are beginning to build smart cities. These are cities where <u>technology</u> and coding will make life easier.

In some smart cities, rubbish is sucked away through pipes and lampposts have cameras in them.

Smart cities will be full of <u>sensors</u>. Messages could be sent to people to tell them about things such as traffic, bad weather and how much electricity and water everyone is using.

In tall buildings, sensors will tell lifts to go to the ground floor when a car arrives outside.

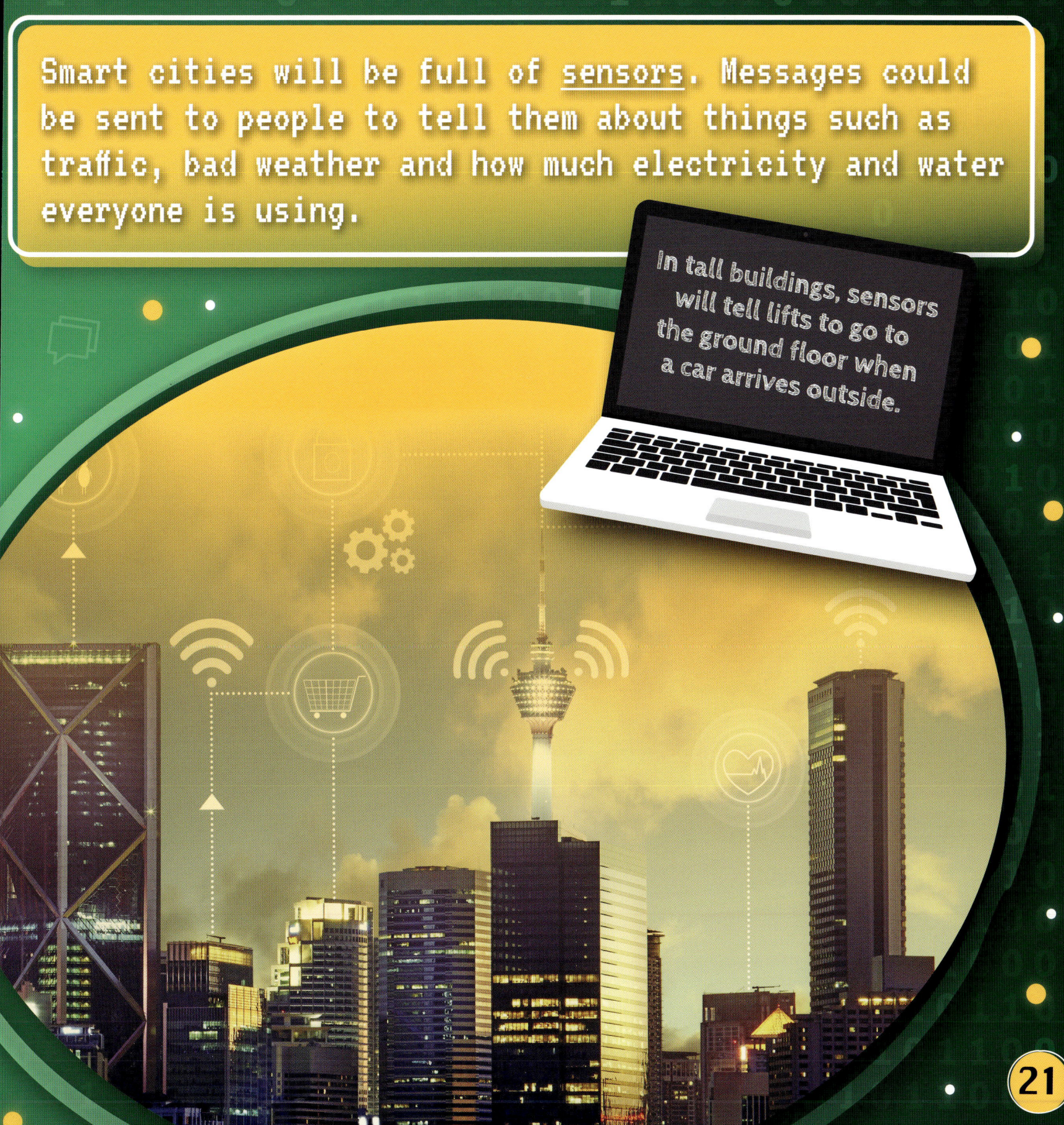

FAMOUS PROGRAMMERS

WINDOW SNYDER

Security Expert

Snyder has worked with lots of big companies to make their code safe from attackers. Attackers try to use code to commit crimes. Snyder tries to stop that from happening.

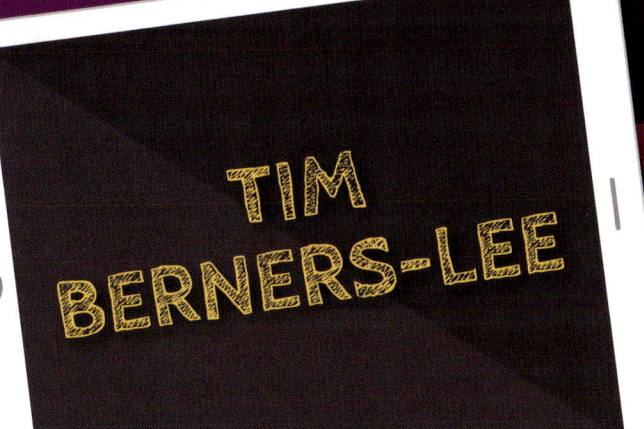

TIM BERNERS-LEE

Inventor of the World Wide Web

The World Wide Web helps connect webpages on the internet together. This is a very important part of the internet. Berners-Lee made sure his World Wide Web was free and able to be used by everybody.

GLOSSARY

accounts	online profiles that are used by one person or a group of people
filter	to remove unwanted things, making searching easier and safer
instructions	a set of steps that explain how something is done
medical	to do with medicine, doctors and hospitals
run	when a computer reads through all the instructions and does what it is told
sensors	technology that can sense things and react to changes
social media	websites and apps that give people a space to make friends and share information about themselves online
store	keep in order to use later
symbols	things that are used as a sign of something else
technology	devices or tools to help us do something

INDEX